Journey to the Center of a Mother

Nicole Strickland

Presentation by *BookLeaf Publishing*

Web: www.bookleafpub.com

E-mail: info@bookleafpub.com

ISBN: 9789395756174

First edition 2022

DEDICATION

To the 18 year olds who didn't want to make it to 24.

To the parents who didn't know if they would make it to 25.

To Eliza - I owe this to you, my number one girl.

ACKNOWLEDGEMENT

Thank you to my family for loving me through every stage of my life. I wouldn't be where I am without.

PREFACE

Being a mom is truly one of the best adventures that you can have, but that doesn't mean that you don't struggle. I love my girls dearly, and I wouldn't trade them for anything, but there are unseen, and seen, struggles that come with being a parent, and I don't want to brush over those.

No one tells you your first break up is the worst one.

You were my whole world.

When you left I had to rediscover that there was beauty without you.

Rebound

I told you to swallow my sorrows, but you only created more.

Savior

A boy in college came over after almost overdosing, and all I could think was how I wanted to save him when I should have been saving myself.

Show Me

Show me your soul.
You don't have to be alone now.
Show me your soul.
All these hidden feelings take their toll.
The sweat is glistening on your brow
I need you to make me a vow.
Show me your soul.

I Thought I Knew...

I thought I knew what love was
until you spit me up,
and left me bleeding on the ground.

I thought I knew what love was
until I saw my dad kiss my mom,
and she wiped off his spit.

I thought I knew what love was
until I drank vodka to erase what was left of you.

10 Things College Taught Me

1. That boy you left back at home will leave you when you make one dumb mistake, leaving you to kiss vodka bottles and the lips of boys who will not remember your last name.

2. "Attendance is mandatory" is what the college will tell you; but there will be days when your arms are weights and your lungs are filled with lead, and there is nothing wrong with that.

3. You are going to drink too much and spend the rest of the night with your head in a bucket crying about a blonde haired boy who doesn't want you anymore…

4. You are going to stare at a bottle of pills and hate yourself because all you want to do is finish the whole damn bottle but you don't have the courage.

Don't.

5. Drugs are going to be in the bloodstream of the boy that you are fucking. Soon you are going to wonder if you are hooked on him or the THC.

...Please don't beg him to stay.

6. Your mother is going to worry. She will ask if your depression is coming back and you are going to lie… But your nights are going to be filled with drunken tears while you beg for the desire to just...live.

7. That boy back at home is going to tell you he still loves you while he is fucking her. It is going to destroy you.

He won't care.

8. Everybody has a vice. Soon cigarettes won't taste at all, and you'll be asking yourself what the ashes would feel like pressed against your skin.

9. You will find your best friend. She will sit with you while your heart breaks and alcohol runs through your veins. She will still love you.

10. You hit rock bottom. It can only go up from here.

Society won't call me pretty anymore...

Tell me that I am pretty,
I know you are going to have to lie.
I know that beautiful things are hard to find.
There are voices in my mind, a personnel
committee,
When they open their mouths, I end up feeling
rather shitty.
I look in the mirror and I want to cry,
He didn't even look me in the eye.
I wish I was born in a different city.

Leaves fall from trees,
like tears from my chin.
Compare me to nature, I might be pretty then.
These thoughts in my brain are like a disease,
they make me want to cut open my skin.
I won't be considered pretty with one scar, not to
mention ten…

Love Me, Please

I
will spend
all my time
explaining the
color of your eyes
to the moon and the stars
If that makes you want to stay.

You

The thing about life,
is that promises get broken.
But please remember:
beautiful things still exist.
I know that, when you are here.

Soulmates

I met you online.
Little did I know,
you would become my lifeline.

We never did say wedding vows…

Hold on to something that will last,
Please ignore my horrific past.
I am not something that will fall,
I promise to give you my all.

I promise you my endless love,
These tears caress my face like doves.
If you answer my pleading call,
I promise to give you my all.

The thing about my heart, my dear,
Its intentions are not that clear.
You make my heartbeat want to stall,
I promise to give you my all.

No one tells you you lose your self postpartum

I am drowning in anger and pain
I can not seem to find my way.
I need someone to help me.
I cannot help myself.
My nightmares haunt me,
they will not fade.
I am scared
to love
you.

Hope

The sun will rise up
After the rain comes falling
Bringing hope for tomorrow

Breathe

I want you to know that you are perfect
That imperfect people do not exist,
and everybody is a little wrecked.
You are not alone with scars on your wrist,
Metal and skin were not meant to connect.
I see you standing there with a red fist.
Anger and madness crawl up your raw throat,
You need it to vanish, so this, I wrote.

Shame

You are not alone in the way you feel shame,
when you raise your voice and holler her name.

You have to remind yourself that she's only a
child,
especially when you have lost yourself in utter
denial.

No one posts of the fucked up head,
the one who brought life, but wishes she was
dead.

You are not alone in the way you feel shame.
You are doing your best, she will love you the
same.

Hidden Denial

17

"Some people just aren't meant to be mothers..."

I nod my head while I agree; all the while knowing, they are talking about me.

Silent Apologies

18

I pick up your sleeping body and tuck it in next to mine.

Hoping this makes you forget when my head wasn't really mine.

Day by Day

I promise I'm fighting against my demons, just
out of sight.
I put them to bed with me every single night
I won't give up, not without a fight.

I promise, my darlings, that we will be alright.